Why My Cat is Better Than Your Ex

(or Your Current)

Standards Raised... By a Feline.

RASHMIE JOY

Made with ❤ on the Notion Press Platform

www.notionpress.com

To Batman—

My midnight singer, slow-blink specialist, and furry relationship guru.

Thank you for modelling how to pursue with grace,

*respect boundaries like a pro, and return—every day—with love in your
eyes and dignity intact.*

You are, without question, the best boyfriend

Contents

In Which a Cat Courts Better Than Most Men I Know

Where Batman Teaches Us That Love Isn't a Chase—It's an Invitation

Where Batman Teaches Us That Rejection Isn't Personal—It's Information

Where Batman Shows Us That Consistency is Romantic, Not Creepy—If You're Not a Jerk About It

Where Batman Shows Us That Consistency is the New Sexy (and Ghosting is Just Emotional Cowardice)

Where Batman Shows Us, That Emotional Literacy is Hotter Than a Six-Pack

Where Batman Teaches Us That Love Without Control is the Only Love That Lasts

Where Batman Teaches Us That Walking Away Isn't Weak—It's Wisdom with Whiskers

Foreword

Most people seek relationship advice from psychologists, therapists, or well-meaning friends.

I got mine from a cat.

Not just any cat—**Batman**, the velvet-pawed, slow-blinking, head-tilting enigma who sauntered into my life like he owned it. A black-furred romantic with yellow eyes that have seen things... and forgiven them anyway.

Batman doesn't speak in words, but his every move is a masterclass in emotional intelligence. He doesn't chase; he approaches. He doesn't demand; he offers. He waits without sulking, persists without pushing, and shows up every single day with the quiet dignity of someone who **knows his worth**—and yet, never imposes it.

In his presence, I began to witness something profound: **a natural blueprint for conscious, respectful, emotionally mature love**.

His interactions with the lady cats—**Daisy, Maple, Chairman Mao, Vivian**—were a medley of charm, rejection, mutual curiosity, and the occasional dramatic swat. But Batman's lessons weren't limited to his feline muses.

He has a **thing for human ladies** too.

His bond with me—the first human he ever allowed to touch him—is tender, deep, and steady. He didn't rush in. He circled, observed, tested trust with caution. He leaned in slowly, blinked deliberately, and one day… allowed his head to rest against my hand.

It wasn't dramatic. It was monumental.

In that moment, I learned that real connection isn't built in declarations—it's built in consistency, respect, and energy. With Batman, I experienced a silent kind of devotion that says, **I see you. I trust you. I'll stay.**

This book was born from that realization.

We're so used to romantic clichés—grand gestures, dramatic declarations, hot-and-cold games. But what if the best love stories are the quieter ones? The kind written in consistent presence, tender glances, shared space, and unspoken respect?

Through Batman, I saw what it means to **pursue without pressure**, to love without possession, and to **hold space without fear**. He taught me that sometimes the best boyfriend isn't the flashiest, or the loudest, or even the most obvious. Sometimes, he's just the one who's **always there**—tail curled, eyes soft, letting you come closer on your own terms.

This is a book about love. But not the love that burns fast and fizzles. This is about **the kind of love that waits on the back step, day after day, trusting you'll open the door.**

Welcome to Batman's world.

You're about to learn from the best.

— Rashmie

Your Self-Mastery & Transformation Architect

(and humble servant to a furry Casanova)

1st April 2025

Preface

This book wasn't part of the plan.

But then again, neither was Batman.

He just showed up one day—silent, observant, black as night, with eyes full of questions and stories he wasn't ready to tell. For weeks, he circled the edges of my life. Watching. Listening. Waiting.

And slowly, with the kind of patience most humans can't even fathom, he began to trust.

First, a glance. Then, a slow blink. Then, one day, he let me pet him. 

And I swear, the earth paused in reverence.

I didn't realize it at the time, but Batman was teaching me something far deeper than animal bonding. He was showing me what healthy, respectful, emotionally intelligent love actually looks like.

Over time, I began to notice how he interacted with the lady cats— each one different in temperament, boundaries, and love languages. Daisy, with her sass and suspicion. Maple, dramatic and territorial. Chairman Mao, feisty yet secretly tender. Vivian, graceful and elusive. And then there was me—his chosen human, the one he allowed into his quiet kingdom.

His behaviour wasn't random. It was… refined.

There was a pattern. A rhythm. A **philosophy**.

And as someone who coaches people on emotional resilience, boundaries, and self-mastery, I couldn't ignore the genius in his simplicity. Here was a cat—untamed, unbothered by social norms, and completely free—modelling better romantic behaviour than most men I'd encountered.

So this book was born—not from theory, but from observation.

From fur and purrs, swats and serenades, patience and presence.

"My Cat is Better Than Your Ex (or Your Current)" is not a relationship manual. It's a collection of stories, reflections, and practical insights wrapped in fur and feline wisdom. It's for anyone who's loved, lost, yearned, misunderstood, or simply wants to love better—with more awareness, more playfulness, and a whole lot more grace.

You'll laugh. You might tear up. You'll definitely see yourself (and your exes) in the characters. But more than anything, I hope you walk away with a new definition of love—one that's rooted in respect, curiosity, boundaries, and being there when it counts.

To Batman, thank you for being my muse, my mirror, and the mentor I never saw coming.

Now go ahead—open your heart, slow blink with intention, and let the Cat King of Romance teach you a thing or two.

Caveat from the Cat-Lady-in-Chief:
Yes, the title says *"boyfriend"*—but don't let that fool you. This book isn't about men vs. women. It's about *relationships vs. emotional intelligence.*
Whether you're dating, married, situationship-ing, or trying to ghost your inner saboteur, this is for **anyone** who wants to love better—and be loved with respect, patience, and presence. Cats don't care about gender. They care about energy. Be like Batman. Watch the energy.

— Rashmie

1st April 2025

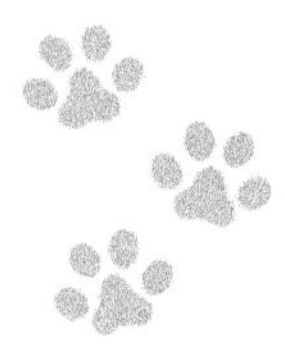

Acknowledgments

To Batman—

My quiet king, my slow-blinking therapist, and the ultimate muse. Thank you for teaching me that love doesn't shout. It shows up, sits beside you, and purrs quietly until you feel safe enough to stay. This book is yours. I just wrote it down.

To Daisy, Maple, Chairman Mao, and Vivian—

Thank you for being the perfect mix of sass, boundaries, mystery, and fire. Your reactions to Batman's romantic advances were the best crash course in relationship psychology I've ever seen. You are divine, unpredictable, and utterly irreplaceable.

To the entire Cat Squad—

For scratching open my heart, teaching me patience, and proving that wisdom sometimes arrives in whiskers and fur.

To the readers—

Whether you picked this book up for fun or stumbled into unexpected truth among the tales—thank you. If this book brings a smile to your face or shifts your view on love even a little, my job is done.

And finally,

To Life, with all its paradoxes and poetry—

Thank you for sending me the teachers I never knew I needed.

With love and purrs,

Rashmie

Prologue/Introduction

In Which a Cat Courts Better Than Most Men I Know

- *"Swipe right? Batman prefers the long game—slow blinks and silent loyalty. Try that on Tinder."*

- *— A very observant human (me)*

Let's face it. Modern relationships are kind of a mess.

And I say this with love. And horror. Mostly horror.

We live in the era of **'connections' without connection**. Ghosting is normal, red flags are romanticized, and people think love is proven by how fast you reply to a text. We've somehow replaced deep courtship with double-taps, real communication with emojis, and unconditional love with, "as long as you meet **my** needs."

It's giving… **fast food romance**.

Quick, hot, cheap—and leaves you emptier than when you started.

Somewhere along the way, we forgot how to love.

How to be kind. How to listen.

How to show up without trying to conquer or control.

How to give space without punishing silence.

How to stay… without staying stuck.

And then—Batman walked in.

A black cat with the swagger of a 90s romantic hero and the emotional intelligence of someone who's definitely done his inner work. He didn't need a dating app. He had **presence**.

He didn't "slide into DMs"—he **slow-blinked from across the compound**.

No drama. No pressure. No emotional blackmail disguised as 'passion.'

Just consistent, respectful, low-key pursuit. And let me tell you… it was magnetic.

Watching him interact with the lady cats was like watching a feline version of **The Notebook**—if Ryan Gosling had whiskers and more patience. Whether it was Daisy's dramatic flair, Maple's diva energy, or Chairman Mao's sass-on-wheels, Batman adapted—not to manipulate, but to harmonize.

He didn't push.

He didn't punish.

He didn't pout.

He waited. He observed. He showed up.

Every. Single. Day.

No expectations. No entitlement. No transactional mindset.

Just presence, play, and gentle persistence.

Now tell me—**how many men (or women, to be fair) do you know who court like that?**

Yeah. Me neither.

This book was born from that contrast. From my utter disbelief that a CAT could demonstrate **more emotional maturity, empathy, and relational grace** than most humans I've seen in therapy, coaching, or couples counselling.

So here's what you can expect:

Each chapter will unpack a real-life moment from Batman's love life—his wins, his losses, his hissing encounters, and his quiet victories.
And through these fur-laced tales, we'll talk about the real stuff:

- How love today has become more about consumption than connection

- Why **space** in a relationship isn't neglect—it's nourishment

- What true courtship looks like when it's not rooted in performance or control

- How giving without agenda is not weakness—it's power

- And how **being present** is sexier than six-pack abs (but I mean, abs are welcome too)

This is not a "how to get the girl / guy" guide.

It's a reminder—served with whiskers and wisdom—that love, when done right, is less about getting and more about **being**.

So If you've ever been ghosted, gaslit, love-bombed, emotionally breadcrumbed, or just generally confused by modern romance…

You're in the right place. And you're in good paws.

Now grab a blanket, sip something warm, and let Batman show you how the real lovers do it—with grace, patience, and the occasional paw to the face.

— Rashmie

Human. Coach. Devoted disciple of the Feline School of Love.

Chapter 1: The Slow Blink of Seduction

Where Batman Teaches Us That Love Isn't a Chase—It's an Invitation

- *"In a world full of chase-and-ghost games, be a slow-blinker."*

- *— Batman (probably)*

Batman doesn't rush.

He doesn't chase, woo loudly, or perform for attention.

He arrives. He observes. He waits. And then—he blinks. Slowly.

With purpose.

It's his signature move.

A soft, subtle, perfectly timed "I see you… but

only if you want to be seen."

Now, if you're not familiar with feline courtship rituals, let me

break it down: the slow blink in cat language is the equivalent of,

"You're safe here. No pressure. Just vibes." It's emotional consent.

A nonverbal offering of presence.

No thirst. No desperation. Just… confidence and calm.

And I've watched this ritual unfold more times than I can count.

There's Daisy—her sass levels peaking, her tail flicking like a

warning siren.

There's Maple—unapologetically dramatic, making everyone work

for her affection.

Chairman Mao—don't even try. She will swat before you finish your sentence.

And Vivian—the distant dreamer, rarely seen, barely touched.

In walks Batman.

Not puffing his chest.

Not yowling for attention.

Just planting himself a respectful few feet away, settling in like a monk meditating under a cherry blossom tree.

And when the time is right…

the blink.

I've watched Daisy glare at him like he owed her money.

I've watched Maple roll her eyes and flop dramatically in the opposite direction.

And I've watched Batman take it all in with zero reaction.

He simply stays. Occasionally blink. Maybe switch paws.

And then—one day—they let him come closer.

Not because he convinced them, manipulated them, or "won" them.

But because he made them feel safe.

What the Slow Blink Really Means

We live in a world that's forgotten the art of slow connection.

Everything is "now."

Love is measured in texting frequency.

Relationships are judged on Instagram-worthy moments.

And if there isn't immediate chemistry, people swipe left—on partners, on potential, on patience.

But love—real love—doesn't start with fireworks.

It starts with nervous system regulation.

With slowness.

With respect for timing, energy, boundaries.

Batman knows this intuitively.

He doesn't rush the process.

He lets the relationship bloom like it's supposed to—in quiet, consistent, curiosity-filled spaces.

The Problem With the Way We "Connect" Today

Let's talk human behaviour for a moment.

Most people today are either:

Performing: "Look at me! Pick me! Validate me!"

Avoiding: "Too vulnerable. Too intense. Too busy. Bye."

Collecting: "Let me have as many 'situationships' as possible just to feel something."

Batman is none of these things.

He doesn't seek validation.

He doesn't run when it gets intimate.

And he doesn't juggle connections for dopamine highs.

He's just… present.

Observing.

Tuned in.

Ready, but not needy.

And that's what makes him magnetic.

The Human Takeaway: *Practice the Slow Blink Rule*

If Batman could give relationship advice (and let's be honest, he already does), here's what he'd teach us:

- Slow down. You don't have to "impress" anyone—just be.

- Be present. Put the phone down. Make eye contact. Breathe.

- Blink slowly (metaphorically or literally). Let people know you're emotionally safe.

- Read the energy, not the ego. If they need space, give it. If they lean in, respond.

- Stop performing. Start being. The right ones will feel your calm before they hear your charm.

Batman's Bonus Tip:

"If she hisses at you today, don't take it personally. Blink. Step back. Come back tomorrow. Or don't. Either way, love her without needing to own her."

In a world full of forced chemistry, fake charm, and fast fades, Batman reminds us that true connection is never rushed.

Sometimes the most seductive thing you can do… is blink slowly, say nothing, and wait near the doorway of someone's heart.

They'll open it when they're ready.

Reflection Zone

Cat vs. Human Comparison Chart

Situation	Batman's Way	Modern Human Dating
Showing interest	Slow, deliberate blinking	Insta-DMs +  emojis
Creating intimacy	Prolonged, patient presence	"So what are we?" on Day 3
Responding to distance	Waits calmly, adjusts proximity	Panic-texts, overthinking, spiraling
Making the first move	Non-verbal cues, no pressure	Grand declarations or awkward memes
Winning affection	Builds trust over time	Seeks instant validation

Thought Prompts & Journaling Cues

When I feel attraction, do I rush into connection or allow space for it to grow?

How do I usually signal interest—and is it rooted in confidence or fear?

What would it feel like to communicate more with presence than with performance?

Can I recall a moment when patience built real connection? What did I learn?

Where in my life do I need to practice "slow blinking"—offering steady, non-demanding attention?

Invitation:

Try the Slow Blink Practice:

The next time you're with someone you care about—friend, partner, cat, or even yourself—pause. Breathe.

Make gentle eye contact.

And blink slowly… as an offering of trust, not expectation.

See what opens up.

Chapter 2: Getting Slapped and Coming Back Anyway

Where Batman Teaches Us That Rejection Isn't Personal—It's Information

- *Not every slap is an attack. Sometimes it's just punctuation."*

- *Daisy, probably after round housing Batman for the third time*

Batman has been slapped.

Not once. Not twice. Many times.

And not the playful kind, either. We're talking full-bodied feline swats with claws partially extended and tails puffed to dramatic proportions.

Now, most tomcats—upon receiving this royal backhand from a female—would retreat. Sulk. Nurse their bruised egos under a car for three days.

Not Batman.

He takes it in stride. One paw back, maybe a blink of confusion, and then—he **sits down**. Calmly. As if to say,

"Message received. Boundaries respected. I'm still here if you ever want to vibe later."

And this… this is why he's better than your ex (or your current).

Let me paint the scene.

It's 6:48 PM—prime dinner hour. Batman appears from the shadows like he's materialized out of the evening mist. Daisy is already at the back door, tail twitching, giving major **"I run this joint"** energy.

He approaches her slowly. A respectful distance.

She hisses. He stops.

She lifts a paw. He lowers his head.

She slaps.

WHACK.

One clean, precise strike to the cheek.

And what does Batman do?

Nothing.

He doesn't hiss back.

He doesn't escalate.

He doesn't storm off or meow dramatically for sympathy.

He **sits down**. One paw tucked in. Tail curled neatly. The embodiment of, **"I still like you. I get that you're not ready. I'll wait over here, no problem."**

He's the Gandhi of romance. With whiskers.

What Most Humans Do Instead

Let's flip the species for a moment.

When people face rejection in dating or relationships today, the default reactions are… not great.

- **Get defensive:** "You're too sensitive."

- **Gaslight:** "Wow, I was just being nice. You're overreacting."

- **Withdraw or punish:** "Fine. Ghosted. Blocked. Good luck."

- **Play the victim:** "No one ever loves me. I try so hard."

Rejection stings.

And when we haven't built emotional resilience or learned how to self-regulate, we lash out.

We make it about us.

We try to control or manipulate the outcome.

We want love—but only if it guarantees our comfort.

Batman says: **"Nope. Love isn't comfort. It's conscious patience."**

What the Paw-Slap Really Means

When Daisy slaps Batman, she's not saying, "I hate you."

She's saying, "Respect my mood."

"Not right now."

"I'm overstimulated."

Or simply: "Back off, Loverboy."

Batman never takes it personally.

Because he's attuned enough to know it's not rejection of **him**—

it's information about **her internal state**.

So he recalibrates. He gives space. He maintains his calm.

And you know what happens?

A few days later, Daisy is rubbing her head against him.

Not because he pushed.

Because he didn't.

The Human Takeaway: *Rejection Is a Mirror, Not a Wall*

Batman's behaviour reminds us that:

- Rejection is often about timing, not worth.

- People need space to feel safe.

- Your reaction to rejection is more telling than the rejection itself.

- Emotional regulation is sexy. Truly.

- Patience without pressure is power.

Why This Matters in the Real World

We're living in a time where vulnerability feels unsafe and boundaries feel like rejection.

Where one "No" can trigger someone's deepest wounds.

Where romantic persistence is often confused with control—or worse, entitlement.

But Batman shows us that **persistence with respect** is a love language of its own.

He doesn't keep trying to push past boundaries.

He just makes it clear: **I'm here. You're safe. And I don't need you to love me back to validate my love.**

Now **that** is the kind of energy we need more of.

Batman's Resilience Rule:

If you get emotionally slapped:

1. Don't retaliate.

2. Don't disappear out of spite.

3. Don't make it about your self-worth.

4. Acknowledge the signal.

5. Sit. Stay. Respect. Reassess.

If they come back later—great.

If not—you still kept your dignity intact and modelled emotional maturity.

In the end, Batman teaches us that true connection isn't about never getting hurt.

It's about not **hurting back**.

It's about being the space someone returns to—not escapes from.

Sometimes the best way to be loved… is to be **so safe, so unshakable, and so centred** that even rejection becomes part of the dance.

Reflection Zone

Cat vs. Human Comparison Chart

Situation	Batman's Way	Typical Human Behaviour
Receiving rejection	Accepts it with grace, no drama	Gets defensive, takes it personally
Coming back after a "No"	Waits, resets energy, tries later	Pushes harder or withdraws completely
Handling emotional boundaries	Reads body language, doesn't insist	Ignores cues, argues, or guilt-trips
Dealing with disappointment	Blinks, flicks tail, finds sun patch	Spirals, vents on WhatsApp, unfollows
Seeking connection again	Shows up calmly when energy is right	Over-explains, over-texts, overthinks

Thought Prompts & Journaling Cues

How do I typically react when I feel rejected—do I shut down or lash out?

When someone sets a boundary with me, do I respect it… or take it as a challenge?

Have I ever come back to someone with softness instead of ego?

What does grace look like for me in moments of emotional disappointment?

Can I create space for people to say "no"—without withdrawing love?

Invitation:

<u>Batman Practice:</u>

The next time someone responds with distance or resistance, try this:

- Pause.
- Observe.
- Blink slowly (literally or emotionally).

Instead of reacting, just be present without needing a response. Let the energy settle. Return when the space feels safe again.

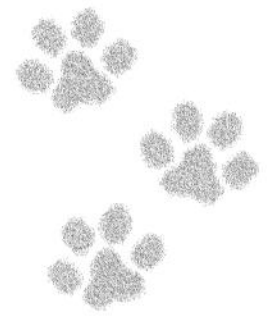

Chapter 3: The Gentle Stalker

Where Batman Shows Us That Consistency is Romantic, Not Creepy—If You're Not a Jerk About It

- *"If you're going to stalk someone, do it with grace, snacks, and emotional neutrality."*
— *Batman, possibly while loitering politely near Maple*

Batman is, by every modern definition, **a stalker**.

But not the creepy, breathing-in-your-DMs-at-2am kind.

No. He's the *gentle stalker*.

He doesn't hover.

He haunts. Softly.

He doesn't follow.

He *appears*. Subtly. Repeatedly. Without expectation.

You could call it loitering with love.

He's *around*, often unseen until you realize he's been sitting behind the potted plant for 45 minutes waiting for your energy to settle.

That's Batman.

Let me give you a classic example.

It's a late evening. The moon's out. The breeze is perfect. Maple has assumed her usual position near the food bowls—tail wrapped around her feet, eyes squinting at anyone who even breathes too loud.

Batman shows up. Doesn't go straight to her.

He walks past the bowls. Sits. Doesn't eat. Just… *places himself in the vicinity of her grace.*

Maple sees him. Of course she does.

He does not approach.

Fifteen minutes pass. He yawns, stretches, blinks.

Maple pretends he doesn't exist.

He shifts slightly closer—half a paw's worth of movement. Not enough to trigger alarm, just enough to register interest.

And then he just *waits*.

By the end of dinner, he's a few feet away. She hasn't hissed. She hasn't cuddled. She hasn't left.

Progress.

This happens every day.

Same ritual. Same rhythm.

Not pushy. Not needy. Not desperate.

Just *there*.

A quiet fixture in her emotional landscape.

Batman plays the long game.

And Maple, the high-boundary queen that she is, starts to soften—

not because he forced her to, but because **his presence became**

predictable in a way that felt safe.

Let's Talk About the Human Equivalent

Here's what many modern relationships look like:

- Day 1: "Hey you're cute."

- Day 2: "You didn't text back. You must not care."

- Day 3: *Blocked.*

- Day 5: "You were the best thing that never happened to me."

- Day 7: New person. New chaos.

We've mistaken **access for intimacy**, and **urgency for**

connection.

But Batman teaches us a subtler truth:

"You don't have to bombard people with attention to matter to them.

You just have to keep showing up the right way."

The Human Takeaway: *Be Consistent Without Being Clingy*

Batman's love language is consistency.

But here's what makes it work: **he's unattached to the outcome.**

He doesn't *need* Maple to respond.

He doesn't spiral if she doesn't reciprocate.

He's just there—softly, calmly, quietly.

Consistency is romantic **only** when it's not transactional.

If you're showing up just to get something in return, you're not loving—you're performing.

What Consistency is NOT:

- It's not love-bombing.

- It's not checking in 18 times a day.

- It's not sulking when they don't respond how you hoped.

- It's not "proving" your value until they finally "choose" you.

That's not courtship. That's coercion.

Batman would never.

Batman's Gentle Stalker Checklist:

1. Be available, not intrusive.

2. Stay calm when unacknowledged.

3. Let their boundaries guide your pace.

4. Never assume closeness entitles you to affection.

5. Return daily with no expectations—just presence.

Why This Matters

In an age of short attention spans and endless swiping, *emotional consistency* is a rare, radiant gem.

But consistency without control? That's sacred.

Batman never shows up to win.

He shows up to witness.

He offers his presence like a gift, not a weapon.

And that's why—even the sassiest of queens like Maple eventually let him stay.

Sometimes the greatest act of love isn't declaring it.

It's simply proving that you *won't disappear the moment things get inconvenient*.

Batman doesn't chase.

He just stays… until staying feels safe.

Reflection Zone

Cat vs. Human Comparison Chart

Situation	Batman's Way	Typical Human Behaviour
Expressing interest	Quietly stays near, observes	Double-texts, Insta-stalks, drops hints
Respecting space	Doesn't intrude—waits for signals	Forces conversations, pops up uninvited
Managing attraction	Lets curiosity guide gentle approach	Chases, over-explains, performs anxiety
Handling indifference	Accepts it, finds other sunbeams	Takes it personally, sulks or obsesses
Making a move	Positions self softly, no pressure	Love-bombs or confesses out of panic

Thought Prompts & Journaling Cues

When I like someone, do I respect their energy—or try to invade it?

Have I mistaken anxiety-fuelled pursuit for romantic interest?

What would it feel like to simply be near someone without expectation?

Where in my life do I need to practice presence instead of performance?

Can I trust connection to unfold without pushing it?

Invitation:

Batman Practice:

Choose one connection—romantic, platonic, or even digital—and pause your usual pursuit pattern.

Instead, tune into your own presence.

Stay curious. Stay near.

Let the other person feel safe enough to move toward you.

Chapter 4: Why Batman Never Ghosts

Where Batman Shows Us That Consistency is the New Sexy (and Ghosting is Just Emotional Cowardice)

> - *"He doesn't vanish when it's inconvenient. He returns when it matters. That's not clingy—that's courage."*
> — *The Human Who's Been Ghosted Enough to Know Better*

Let's get this out of the way:

Batman is not a ghoster.

He has too much dignity. Too much emotional intelligence. And

frankly, too much fur to vanish like that.

He doesn't disappear mid-conversation.

He doesn't stop showing up because he

didn't get the response he wanted.

He doesn't emotionally retreat when things

get real.

He just keeps showing up—without noise, without drama, and

without making it *your job* to chase him.

Even when Chairman Mao ignores him.

Even when Maple rolls her eyes so hard you can hear it.

Even when Daisy hisses like she's channelling her inner dragon…

Batman doesn't bail.

He recalibrates. He gives space. And then, when the time feels

right, he's *back*.

Calm. Quiet. Steady.

He's emotionally *available*. And you know what?

That's rare. And it's hot.

Meanwhile, in the Human World...

Ah yes, ghosting—the ultimate love trick of the emotionally

unequipped.

The act of vanishing without a word.

No closure. No clarity. Just… radio silence and a cold, "maybe I dreamt the whole connection?" panic spiral.

Ghosting is the modern equivalent of slamming a door without ever acknowledging there *was* a door.

And it's become disturbingly normal.

We ghost because:

- We don't want to deal with discomfort.

- We can't handle emotional accountability.

- We think silence is easier than honesty.

- Or worse—we're afraid to be the "bad guy," so we become the invisible one instead.

But here's the truth:

Disappearing doesn't make you kind. It makes you avoidant.

Batman's Approach: The Return Ritual

Batman never ghosts because he never *pretends* to be something he's not.

- If he's interested, he shows up.

- If he's not sure, he observes.

- If he senses tension, he gives space—but stays nearby.

- And when the energy feels open again? He's back. Just like that.

No passive-aggression.

No withdrawal games.

No "read receipts" followed by weeks of

silence.

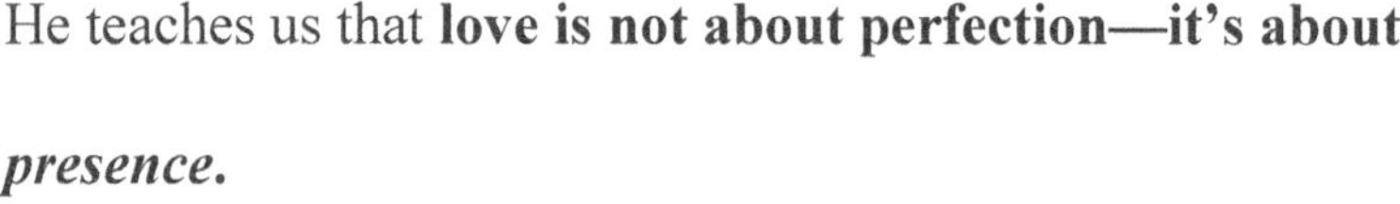

He teaches us that **love is not about perfection—it's about**

presence.

Even if you messed up.

Even if there was conflict.

Even if there's awkwardness.

You can always return. Gently. Honestly. Without ego.

The Human Takeaway: *Ghosting Is a Symptom of Fear, Not Freedom*

Batman teaches us that:

- You don't have to flee just because it's complicated.

- You're allowed to be uncertain—but don't disappear in the process.

- People remember who stayed when it was messy.

- Emotional maturity looks like *showing up even when it's awkward*.

Batman's No-Ghosting Code:

1. **Leave when needed—but say so.** Don't vanish. Communicate.

2. **Silence is sacred, not weaponized.** Don't use it to punish.

3. **Return gently.** Without excuses. Without expectation.

4. **Let presence speak louder than explanation.**

5. **Be reliable. Especially when no one's watching.**

Because Sometimes, the Return is the Romance

When Batman shows up again after days of distance, he doesn't meow like a martyr.

He doesn't demand attention.

He simply places himself within view, offers a slow blink, and waits.

And somehow, that silent return feels more intimate than a thousand apologies.

Because true love doesn't always need words.

Sometimes it just needs proof that **you didn't disappear when it was hard.**

In the end, Batman reminds us:

You don't need the perfect comeback line.

You don't need a dramatic reconciliation.

You just need to *be there*—when it counts, when it's quiet, when it's not easy.

So stop ghosting. Be a Batman.

The world doesn't need another emotionally unavailable Houdini.

It needs a black-furred legend who shows up, sits down, and says

with his eyes: *"I'm still here, if you are."*

Reflection Zone

Cat vs. Human Comparison Chart

Situation	Batman's Way	Typical Human Behaviour
Feeling overwhelmed	Steps back quietly, then returns	Disappears without explanation (ghosts)
Ending a connection	Loiters respectfully, allows space	Avoids, blocks, vanishes
Taking time for self	Withdraws with grace, stays emotionally present	Leaves without closure
Communication rhythm	Consistent in energy, even when silent	Hot and cold—confusing signals
Reconnecting	Returns softly, no drama or guilt	Sends random meme at 2AM, expects applause

Thought Prompts & Journaling Cues

When I need space, do I communicate— or disappear?

Have I ghosted someone because I feared discomfort or vulnerability?

What does emotional consistency look like for me in relationships?

How can I return with integrity, instead of hiding behind silence?

Who in my life deserves a soft re-entry instead of avoidance?

Invitation:

Batman Practice:

Before you withdraw from someone, pause.

Ask yourself: Can I leave with care?

A simple, honest message—"I need space, but I'll return"—is more healing than silence.

Be the soft place someone remembers, not the vanishing act they never understood.

Chapter 5: Tail Flicks & Emotional Signals

Where Batman Shows Us, That Emotional Literacy is Hotter Than a Six-Pack

-    *"She didn't say she was mad. Her tail said it. And I listened."*
    — Batman, Emotional Support Cat & Feline Empath

Let's talk about **tail flicks**.

To the untrained eye, it might look like Maple is just flicking her tail to swat a mosquito or stretch her hips.

But Batman knows better.

He knows a tail flick is never *just* a tail flick.

It's a message. A whole *emotional monologue*. And baby, he's fluent in **tail dialect**.

- A slow flick = mild irritation.

- A sharp swish = "Back off, Casanova."

- A puffed tail = "You better teleport elsewhere immediately."

- No tail movement + wide eyes = "You may approach… but mess it up, and you die."

Batman doesn't guess.

He *reads*.

He adjusts.

And most importantly—**he doesn't argue with the energy.**

Meanwhile, in the Human Realm...

You know what humans do when they get emotional signals?

Ignore them.

"Oh, she said she's tired. But she laughed at my joke, so she must want to talk."

"He said he's overwhelmed but still posted on Instagram. That means he's ignoring me, right?"

"She didn't reply for two hours. She's probably cheating."

"He sighed during dinner. But it's fine. He'll get over it."

We don't read energy. We project intentions.

We don't ask. We assume.

We don't regulate. We react.

And this, dear reader, is why couples argue over *nothing* and miss *everything*.

Batman's Approach: Observe First. Move Later.

Batman doesn't assume he's always welcome—even when he's been invited in before.

Each interaction is a fresh emotional moment.

He checks the vibes before taking a step.

If Daisy's ears are tilted sideways, he doesn't try to rub up against her.

If Maple's tail is doing the "Don't you dare" cha-cha, he stays still.

If Chairman Mao is frozen in that majestic *"I'll allow it"* pose, he proceeds slowly… respectfully… with blink-offering dignity.

He gets it: **today's yes doesn't guarantee tomorrow's yes**.

Because people (and cats) are emotional landscapes—ever shifting, always communicating.

You just have to learn to listen without demanding subtitles.

The Human Takeaway: *Emotional Intelligence Is More Than Just "Being Nice"*

Real emotional intelligence means:

- Noticing micro-signals

- Responding, not reacting

- Making space for shifting emotions

- Respecting non-verbal boundaries

- Not forcing someone to explain what they're already showing you

Batman is a walking (okay—gliding) example of this.

He watches. He waits. He calibrates.

He doesn't take things personally because he *pays attention.*

Batman's Emotional Intelligence Checklist:

1. **Look before you leap.** Observe body language, tone, and vibes before initiating intimacy.

2. **Don't assume access is permanent.** Emotional states fluctuate. Respect that.

3. **Respond to signals—not your ego.**

4. **Give space when you sense friction.**

5. **Let comfort be the invitation—not just consent.**

Human Translation:

If someone seems off—**don't bulldoze them with expectations or questions.**

Just offer gentle presence. Ask softly. Back off respectfully. Stay emotionally *available*, not emotionally *invasive*.

If Batman can read the room *without* a shared language…

we, with all our words and tools, can surely

manage a bit of attunement.

Final Thoughts:

Sometimes the most powerful thing you can do in love is…

nothing.

Just sit. Wait. Blink.

And listen to what their energy is whispering—*not* what your fear

is screaming.

Batman doesn't decode tail flicks to manipulate.

He reads them to understand.

And that's why—even the fiercest of felines eventually soften in

his presence.

Reflection Zone

Cat vs. Human Comparison Chart

Situation	Batman's Way	Typical Human Behaviour
Feeling annoyed	Flicks tail, turns slightly away	Says "I'm fine" but radiates fury
Overstimulated	Walks off, finds a quiet spot	Snaps, sulks, or lashes out
Feeling safe	Lays nearby, slow blinks	May not know how to show it
Setting a boundary	A look, a hiss, or a tail-twitch	Avoids the convo or explodes
Emotional cues	Clear, physical, and honest	Passive-aggressive, over-analytical

Thought Prompts & Journaling Cues

How do I usually signal my emotional state—clearly or confusingly?

What "tail flick" signs does my body give before I explode?

Do I expect people to read my mind, or do I express my needs directly?

How can I develop my own emotional signal language—without guilt or fear?

Have I ignored someone else's nonverbal signals because I wanted a different answer?

Invitation:

Batman Practice:

Pay attention to your own tail flicks this week—your posture, tone, breath, and inner tension.

Catch the micro-signal before it becomes a full-blown hiss.

And when you notice someone else subtly shifting? Respond with curiosity instead of assumption.

Chapter 6: My Way or the Highway? Batman Disagrees

Where Batman Teaches Us That Love Without Control is the Only Love That Lasts

> - *"You can't force closeness and call it connection. Real love walks beside—it doesn't drag behind."*
> — *Batman, King of Graceful Relationships*

If Batman had a dating profile, under "relationship style" it would say:

"Flexible. Non-controlling. Will adjust purring volume as needed."

What it would *not* say is:

"My way or the highway."

"Take it or leave it."

"Either you do what I want or this isn't going to work."

Why?

Because Batman isn't into ultimatums.

He's into *understanding*.

He's not looking for power. He's looking

for *presence*.

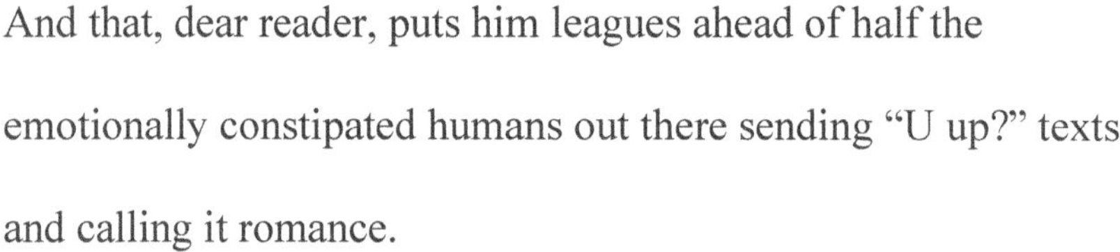

And that, dear reader, puts him leagues ahead of half the emotionally constipated humans out there sending "U up?" texts and calling it romance.

The Modern Ego-Driven Relationship Template:

- "If you can't give me what I want, I'm out."

- "I told you I need XYZ, and if you don't deliver, we're done."

- "I don't have time to explain myself—you either get it, or you don't."

- "I don't believe in compromise. I know my worth."

- "It's not me, it's your inability to meet my standards."

(Translation: It's you.)

We've mistaken **rigidity for strength**, and **entitlement for self-respect.**

But Batman knows better.

The Batman Way: Compromise Without Losing Self

Let's talk about Daisy.

She's a diva. A queen. A swatter of bold tomcats and an artist of the dramatic walkaway.

Batman? He *adores* her.

But he never corners her.

Never guilt-trips her.

Never tries to "train" her out of her boundaries.

He simply adapts.

If she prefers to eat 3 feet away—he places himself 4 feet away.

If she hisses at him when he sits too close—he shifts back, no resentment.

If she ignores him completely—he gives her space, and returns later like nothing happened.

And slowly, magically, she softens.

Because there's no pressure. No ego.

Just presence. Respect. Choice.

The Human Takeaway: *True Love Doesn't Issue Threats*

Real partnership doesn't say:

"You'd better change, or I'm leaving."

It says:

"I see you. I hear you. Can we meet in the middle without erasing ourselves?"

Batman never asks Daisy to be *less Daisy* in order to feel loved. And that's why she eventually lets him close.

What's Happening Emotionally Here?

What Batman models is **secure attachment.** He's:

- Self-assured but not controlling

- Emotionally flexible but not passive

- Grounded in his worth, so he doesn't require others to validate it

He creates space for others to show up as they are—not as who he wants them to be.

Batman's Relationship Rules for Letting Go of Control:

1. You don't have to win to be worthy.

2. Flexibility isn't weakness—it's wisdom.

3. Your partner is not your puppet.

4. Power plays ruin real connection.

5. Boundaries aren't barriers—they're invitations to learn trust.

Closing Reflection:

Too many relationships today feel like negotiations in a boardroom.

Who's giving more? Who's getting their way?

Who's in charge of making the other person feel okay?

But love isn't about being *right*.

It's about being *real*.

Batman teaches us that when you drop the ego, drop the need to control, drop the scripted expectations—something better rises in its place:

Mutuality. Curiosity. Grace.

A love that bends without breaking.

A love that adapts without vanishing.

A love that stays… without needing to stay *in charge*.

Reflection Zone

Cat vs. Human Comparison Chart

Situation	Batman's Way	Typical Human Behaviour
Disagreeing with a partner	Steps back, observes, recalibrates	Doubles down, dominates the conversation
Not getting his way	Waits for a better opening	Pouts, argues, threatens to walk away
Navigating different needs	Adjusts proximity and presence	Demands compromise immediately
Respecting individuality	Gives space without resentment	Tries to "fix" or control the other
Handling tension	Withdraws peacefully, returns in calm	Reacts defensively or emotionally shuts down

Thought Prompts & Journaling Cues

When I don't get my way, how do I usually respond—pause or push?

Do I make space for disagreement without making it personal?

How do I handle it when someone close to me doesn't choose "my way"?

What would it look like to lovingly step back, instead of insisting?

Is my idea of "compromise" actually just quiet control?

Invitation:

Batman Practice:

Next time you hit a moment of tension or misalignment, don't try to fix it immediately.

Pause. Shift your energy.

Loiter calmly like Batman.

Let the other person feel safe enough to meet you halfway—without force, without fear.

Chapter 7: When to Sit, When to Stroll

Where Batman Teaches Us That Walking Away Isn't Weak—It's Wisdom with Whiskers

> - *"Sometimes the most powerful move in love… is the quiet retreat."*
> — *Batman, Master of the Strategic Exit*

There's a moment—after the 7th hiss, the second swat, and the

deep soul-stare of *"try me and die"*—when Batman knows it's

time.

He doesn't argue.

He doesn't plead.

He doesn't create drama or hold a press conference.

He just… strolls away.

Calmly. Smoothly. With quiet dignity.

Not storming off like he's making a point.

Not sulking in the shadows waiting for

someone to chase him.

Just a low-key, graceful disengagement that says:

"Right now, your energy doesn't feel safe. I'll catch you later."

And he means it.

Sometimes he's back the next day.

Sometimes next week.

Sometimes he finds a sunnier ledge and naps instead.

But he always exits with elegance.

The Batman Exit Strategy:

A Masterclass in Emotional Self-Respect

Unlike most humans who panic when met with discomfort—

Batman doesn't see walking away as rejection.

He sees it as **redirection**.

If the vibes are off, he leaves.

Not out of pettiness, not to "teach a lesson,"

but simply because **he respects the**

emotional climate enough to not try and

force sunshine into a thunderstorm.

Meanwhile, in the Human Realm...

Here's what usually happens when people feel tension or

resistance:

- They **push harder**: "Why are you pulling away? Talk to

  me!"

- They **emotionally spiral**: "You're leaving because I'm not

  enough!"

- They **cling tighter**: "If I just do more, say more, *love* more,

  they'll stay…"

- Or they do the worst one: the **passive-aggressive martyr exit**:

"Fine. I guess I'm the only one who cares." (*slams door*)

Spoiler alert: none of these are effective.

They're reactions rooted in **fear**, not clarity.

Batman doesn't do fear-based behavior.

He does *feline boundaries with Buddha-level detachment.*

Human Takeaway: *Know When to Sit. Know When to Stroll.*

There's wisdom in knowing:

- When presence heals

- When silence soothes

- When space is sacred

- And when trying harder is actually hurting more

You don't have to abandon people.

But you *can* remove your energy temporarily when the moment calls for it.

And you can do it *without making it a power move.*

Batman's Graceful Exit Guide:

1. **Pause before pushing.** Is your presence helping or triggering more tension?

2. **Watch for body-language boundaries.** The emotional weather is always visible.

3. **Retreat without resentment.** Leave without blame, shame, or guilt.

4. **Don't make your exit a statement.** Make it a *response.*

5. **Return only when the space feels safe again.** You're not a fixer—you're a feeler.

The Deeper Lesson

So many of us were taught that *staying* is the only proof of love.

That walking away means you gave up.

But what if walking away, at the right time, with the right

energy… is actually **an act of love**?

Love for the other person's space.

Love for your own peace.

Love for the relationship's long-term health.

Batman knows this.

He's not afraid to take his tail elsewhere when the room isn't

ready.

And somehow—*miraculously*—he's often welcomed back even

warmer than before.

Why?

Because he never left with bitterness.

He left with grace.

Sometimes, the kindest thing you can do for a relationship is to **give it air**.

To walk—not because you're done…

But because **you trust the connection enough to pause**.

Batman doesn't slam doors.

He just strolls… and circles back when the energy is right.

And that, my friend, is romantic emotional intelligence in its purest, paw-iest form.

Reflection Zone

Cat vs. Human Comparison Chart

Situation	Batman's Way	Typical Human Behaviour
When connection feels off	Pauses, watches energy shift	Overanalyses, clings harder
Not being welcomed	Leaves quietly, without drama	Gets defensive, demands closure
Sensing emotional misalignment	Adjusts rhythm, strolls elsewhere	Tries to force a conversation or fix it
Letting go	Walks away with calm dignity	Spirals, stalks socials, reopens wounds
Trusting return	Believes in shared rhythm over control	Feels rejected, creates chaos

Thought Prompts & Journaling Cues

How do I handle it when someone pulls away emotionally or physically?

Do I know when to sit with something—and when to stroll away?

Have I ever stayed too long in a space where I wasn't emotionally safe?

What does walking away with grace look like for me?

Can I trust that what's meant for me will find me—even if I pause?

Invitation:

Batman Practice:

Notice where in your life you're forcing movement when what you really need is stillness.

And notice where you're sitting in discomfort when your heart already knows it's time to stroll.

Practice pausing—not to manipulate or test—but to reset your centre.

Chapter 8: The Power of Waiting Near the Door

Where Batman Teaches Us That Love Doesn't Force Entry—It Waits for an Invitation

> - *"He didn't scratch. He didn't cry. He didn't leave.*
> *He just waited near the door like it might open—not for him, but*
> *because it's time."*
> *— Me, forever humbled by a black-furred Zen master*

It's 7:02 PM.

Batman is not on the ledge.

He is not at the food bowl.

He is… at the door. Sitting. Silent. Poised.

He's not meowing.

He's not pacing.

He's not throwing himself dramatically against the grill like a rejected soap opera hero.

He's just there.

Not staring at the door.

Not staring at me.

Just present, softly gazing into the dusk like he knows—*if the door is meant to open, it will.*

And this is where Batman shows us one of the most graceful love skills of all:

How to wait without pressure.

The Spiritual Energy of Space-Holding

Batman doesn't "wait" the way most of us do.

He doesn't fidget, fume, or anxiously overthink.

He doesn't keep score.

He doesn't "wait" to get something.

He simply *is*.

He's a presence. A quiet witness.

An invitation, not an imposition.

You can feel him near you—not heavy, not clingy, just *there*.

And because there's no pressure, no agenda, **you feel safe to open up** when you're ready.

And when you do—he doesn't celebrate like he's won something. He just softly steps in, like, *"Of course. I knew you would when you were ready."*

And isn't that what we're all secretly craving?

Someone who doesn't try to fix us…

doesn't try to force us…

just **waits near the door**, heart open, ego shut?

Meanwhile, in the Human Realm…

Waiting near the door? Oh no, we don't do that. We do:

- **Constant texting:** "Are you okay? Are we okay? You haven't replied. I'm freaking out."

- **Passive-aggressive silence:** "Fine. I'll leave you alone forever. Hope you're happy."

- **Control disguised as care:** "I just want to know how I can *help* you open up…" (*translation: "Hurry up and be okay again so I feel safe."*)

We don't wait.

We chase.

We press.

We panic.

Because we mistake someone's quiet for rejection…

when often, it's just **their nervous system needing a minute.**

Batman's Way: Presence Without Pressure

Batman's quiet vigil by the door is a lesson in:

- **Emotional sovereignty** – He holds his ground without invading yours.

- **Energetic restraint** – He doesn't demand attention. He magnetizes it.

- **Confidence without neediness** – He trusts the door will open, or he'll find another one.

And that confidence?

That non-clingy consistency?

That's what creates trust.

Human Takeaway: *Learn to Stay Without Clinging*

Here's what we can all learn from Batman:

- Your partner's silence isn't always about you.

- Waiting doesn't mean being passive—it means being attuned.

- Love that pressures is not love—it's anxiety dressed in emotional armour.

- Your energy at the metaphorical "door" matters more than the words you shout through it.

- Sometimes, you just need to be the *calmest presence in the room*—and let the door open when it's ready.

Batman's Sacred Space-Holding Guide:

1. Don't hover. Just be near.

2. No chasing. No fixing. No nudging.

3. Energetic stability over emotional noise.

4. Respect the door. Don't pick the lock.

5. Let your presence say, "I'm here, when you are."

Batman's Sacred Space-Holding Guide:

Final Reflection

In a world obsessed with *action*, Batman teaches us the rare power of *being still*.

To wait without drama.

To love without demand.

To hold space without making it about us.

To understand that sometimes, the most sacred thing you can offer someone is **your unflinching, quiet presence at the edge of their emotional threshold**.

Batman doesn't just wait near doors.

He becomes the reason you eventually feel safe enough to open them.

Reflection Zone

Cat vs. Human Comparison Chart

Situation	Batman's Way	Typical Human Behaviour
Desiring closeness	Sits nearby, leaves the door emotionally open	Pushes for connection or demands access
Sensing someone's need for space	Steps back, stays within energetic reach	Misreads as rejection and overreacts
Being patient	Waits calmly, no countdown or conditions	Builds resentment or tests the other person
Respecting privacy	Doesn't enter unless invited	Oversteps, over-questions, over-texts
Offering presence	Offers calm availability, not pressure	Weaponizes silence or proximity

Thought Prompts & Journaling Cues

How comfortable am I sitting in emotional waiting rooms—with no guarantee?

When someone needs space, do I withdraw in fear—or wait with grace?

Where in my relationships can I offer proximity without expectation?

What does consensual connection feel like—and am I practicing it?

Have I respected my own boundaries as much as I try to respect others'?

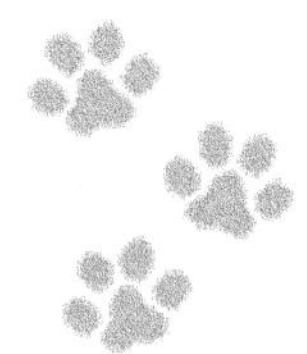

Invitation:

Batman Practice:

Practice being near without hovering—physically or emotionally.

If someone needs space, try saying:

"I'm around. No pressure."

Then mean it.

Trust that doors, when left respectfully unknocked, open from the inside.

Chapter 9: Why Batman Doesn't Love-Bomb

Where Batman Teaches Us That Steady Love is Stronger Than Sudden Intensity

- *"If someone shows up with fireworks and vanishes by sunrise, that's not love—it's a performance. Batman prefers candles to explosions."*
— Your local emotional arson survivor (also me)

Love-bombing is all the rage these days.

And by "rage," I mean actual *rage-inducing behaviour* disguised as romance.

First, they flood you with attention.

Then, they smother you with affection.

Then, they start talking soulmates and

synchronizing Spotify playlists by Day 3.

It's overwhelming, intoxicating, and often… **unsustainable**.

Because love-bombing isn't love.

It's **emotional overcompensation with a side of anxious attachment and hidden control issues.**

Now, let's contrast that with Batman.

Batman doesn't show up with grandeur.

No sudden leaps into your space. No grand declarations. No midnight serenades on rooftops with a harmonica.

He just arrives.

Soft. Steady. Silent.

Like the moonlight. Or emotional intelligence in fur.

The Batman Love Vibe

When Batman starts getting curious about someone—Daisy, Maple, or even me—he doesn't burst in with *"I LOVE YOU PLEASE NOTICE ME."*

He:

- Positions himself a little closer than yesterday

- Blinks slowly, consistently

- Waits for your energy to shift

- Offers quiet company, then gives space

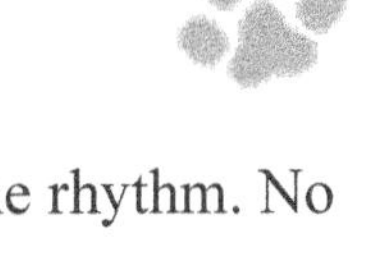

- Returns the next day. Same time. Same rhythm. No pressure

No grand entrances. No emotional rollercoasters.

Just gentle, respectful connection that **builds over time**.

And you know what?

It's wildly comforting.

Meanwhile, in the Human World…

Love-bombing gets mistaken for "romantic intensity."

But here's what it really is:

- "You're perfect. I've never felt this way before!" (*...after two days? Okay.*)

- Excessive texting, calling, messaging, planning

- Talking about the future before understanding the present

- Flooding you with validation and disappearing the moment you set a boundary

- Expecting reciprocation for their affection, instantly

Love-bombers create **emotional debt**.

Batman creates **emotional safety**.

Big difference.

Human Takeaway: *Choose Stability Over Stimulation*

Batman reminds us:

- Love isn't proven by speed. It's proven by **presence.**

- Intensity is not intimacy.

- Romance doesn't have to be explosive to be powerful.

- If someone's energy crashes in hard, ask yourself: *Can they stay soft? Can they stay at all?*

The healthiest love often feels… boring.

Calm. Quiet. Predictable in the best way.

That's not a lack of spark.

That's **your nervous system not being in a**

panic spiral.

Batman's Anti-Love-Bombing Code:

1. Start slow. Let curiosity lead.

2. Keep your rhythm steady, not showy.

3. Let trust build instead of forcing closeness.

4. Avoid over-promising and under-delivering.

5. Focus on connection, not performance.

Bonus: The Burnout of Love-Bombing

People who love-bomb are often unconsciously terrified of:

- Being alone

- Not being "enough" without the drama

- Losing control

- Being vulnerable without the cushion of intensity

But Batman? He's not afraid of silence.

He doesn't need to dazzle to be loved.

He simply **is**, and lets love find its natural

flow.

Final Reflection

A love that erupts often also **evaporates**.

But a love that *settles in slowly, safely, soulfully*?

That's the kind of love that stays.

Batman may not bring flowers.

But he brings consistency.

He brings attunement.

He brings a calm that says: *"I'll still be here tomorrow. And the next day. And the next."*

And honestly?

That's the real love bomb we all need.

Reflection Zone

Cat vs. Human Comparison Chart

Situation	Batman's Way	Typical Human Behaviour
Meeting someone new	Approaches slowly, reads the room	Comes in hot with declarations & gifts
Offering affection	Gentle head bumps, soft purrs	Overwhelms with intensity + over-sharing
Building trust	One blink at a time	Demands closeness early
Handling resistance	Pauses, reassesses vibe	Pushes harder or gets insecure
Showing love	Quiet loyalty, daily presence	Grand gestures followed by withdrawal

Thought Prompts & Journaling Cues

Do I tend to lead with intensity or steady presence in relationships?

How do I respond when someone doesn't return my affection right away?

Have I ever mistaken fast closeness for real connection?

What does it look like to love someone without trying to win them over?

How can I shift from proving love to offering it calmly and consistently?

Invitation:

Batman Practice:

The next time you feel the urge to go "all in" too fast—pause.

Try building connection through quiet gestures: thoughtful texts, soft check-ins, or even silence filled with care.

Let love bloom at its own pace.

Batman never rushes affection… and somehow, everyone still ends up loving him.

Chapter 10: The Purr Heard 'Round the World

Where Batman Teaches Us That You Don't Have to Fix Them—You Just Have to Stay

- *"He didn't try to solve anything. He just purred. And somehow, that was enough."*
— Me, after being emotionally stabilized by a four-legged therapist

Some days are heavier than others.

There are days when everything feels like static in your soul.

When no words make sense.

When your mind is fried and your heart feels like a tangled ball of yarn—chewed up, spit out, and slightly damp with disappointment.

And on those days… Batman shows up.

He doesn't do anything dramatic.

No loud meows. No pawing at the door. No rubbing aggressively against your leg like he's emotionally caffeinated.

He just finds a spot near you and **purrs**.

Not loudly. Not performatively.

Just a steady, soft, rhythmic vibration that feels like the emotional equivalent of a deep exhale.

And suddenly, without solving a single problem or offering any advice, **you feel better.**

That's Batman.

The king of *presence over performance*.

The Healing Power of Silent Companionship

We live in a world where people think *"being there"* means

having the right words.

We're obsessed with advice.

Fixing.

Analysing.

Problem-solving.

But when someone's hurting, overwhelmed, or lost in their own emotional fog—they don't need a rescue.

They need a witness.

Someone to sit beside their sorrow without trying to shrink it.

Someone who says with their energy, not their words:

"You're not alone. I've got you. Feel it all. I'm not going anywhere."

Batman doesn't rescue me from pain.

He doesn't try to distract me.

He just sits there, vibrating gently, letting

his stillness settle something in me that no

sentence ever could.

Meanwhile, in the Human World...

Here's what we often do when someone we love is down:

- **"Let me cheer you up!"** (a.k.a. *deny their emotion*)

- **"Have you tried journaling, yoga, spirulina smoothies?"** (unsolicited solution spam)

- **"You'll be fine. It's just a phase."** (aka: emotional gaslighting, but with a hug)

Our intentions are good.

But what we often forget is:

People don't want to be fixed. They want to feel safe enough to fall apart.

Batman gets this.

He doesn't say, "Cheer up!"

He doesn't Google solutions.

He just purrs. And purrs. And *lets your nervous system remember what safety feels like.*

Human Takeaway: *Your Presence is More Powerful Than Your Advice*

The next time someone you love is hurting, try this:

- Don't interrupt their silence.

- Don't offer ten-step plans.

- Just sit. Softly. Gently.

- Offer your breath. Your attention.

- If it feels right, place your hand over theirs and simply say, *"I'm here."*

It's not dramatic.

But it's **deeply, soulfully healing**.

Batman's Sacred Support Code:

1. Be the calm, not the commentary.

2. Touch only if invited. Purr metaphorically if you must.

3. Hold space like a Zen master—quiet, nonjudgmental, steady.

4. Trust that your presence alone is enough.

5. Be someone who makes others feel emotionally *safe*, not emotionally *corrected*.

Bonus: Co-Regulation, Cat Style

What Batman does when he purrs isn't just cute—it's

neurobiological magic.

His presence:

- Regulates my breathing

- Grounds my racing thoughts

- Sends my nervous system signals of safety

- Reminds my body that not everything is a threat

He co-regulates.

Without saying a word.

And if a cat can do that with a heartbeat and a purr, imagine what we can do with intention and presence.

Final Reflection

In a world that equates love with action, Batman reminds us that sometimes, **love is stillness**.

Love is knowing when not to speak.

Love is sitting beside the broken pieces—not to sweep them up, but to say, *"I'm not afraid of your mess."*

His purr is not a solution.

It's a **song of solidarity**.

And sometimes… that's all we need.

Reflection Zone

Cat vs. Human Comparison Chart

Situation	Batman's Way	Typical Human Behaviour
Seeing someone in pain	Sits close, offers quiet purring	Tries to "fix it" or talk too much
Offering support	Presence, touch, slow blink	Advice, distraction, or performance
Handling vulnerability	Becomes softer, not louder	Feels awkward or retreats
Co-regulating emotion	Calms others through stillness	Mirrors anxiety or shuts down
Being a safe space	Makes room without invading	Overpromises, underdelivers

Thought Prompts & Journaling Cues

When someone I care about is struggling, do I show up with presence—or pressure?

Have I ever felt deeply supported by someone's quiet, nonverbal love?

What are my own "purrs"—small ways I offer emotional safety without needing to speak?

Can I sit with someone's pain without trying to fix it?

How do I co-regulate with people I love? What could I do more gently?

Invitation:

<u>Batman Practice:</u>

This week, show up for someone without trying to fix, solve, or soothe with noise.

Sit close. Let your calm speak louder than any speech.

Sometimes, love isn't about what we say—it's about who we're willing to sit beside… quietly, purring inside.

Chapter 11: Loyalty Without Leashes

Where Batman Teaches Us That Real Love Lets You Roam—And Trusts You'll Return

> - *"She comes. She goes. I stay.*
> *Not because she's mine. Because I choose to."*
> — Batman, *Feline Zen Master of Detachment*

There's something quietly powerful about the way Batman loves.

He's loyal—not because he demands exclusivity, but because **he feels no need to chase what is meant to stay**.

He doesn't need a leash.

He doesn't need constant validation.

He doesn't guard or gatekeep or stalk with desperation.

He's there—every day, same spot, same blink, same soft presence.

But if Daisy, or Maple, or Chairman Mao decides to walk away, he

lets them go.

Not with bitterness.

Not with a guilt-trip stare.

Just with quiet acknowledgment.

Almost like he's saying: *"Go be free. I'll be here when you need stillness again."*

And they almost always come back.

Because that kind of love?

It's magnetic.

Meanwhile, in the Human Realm...

The moment we feel affection, attraction, or intimacy…

we panic.

We start to **cling**.

We text more.

We question everything.

We ask for labels, reassurance, GPS tracking (emotionally, of course).

And when our partner pulls back or takes space?

We spiral.

Why?

Because many of us equate *closeness* with *control*.

But Batman? He's here to say:

"Let them go. Let them roam. Love isn't a leash—it's a lighthouse."

The Batman Way: Devotion with Freedom

When Batman shows up, he shows up.

Fully. Calmly. With all his velvet-coated attention.

But he doesn't chase.

He doesn't follow others from rooftop to rooftop.

He doesn't cry when they walk away.

He doesn't compete.

He just *waits*.

Because his loyalty isn't about ownership.

It's about **choice**.

Every day, he chooses to return to the same space.

Not because he's tied down.

But because he's anchored.

Human Takeaway: *Possession Is Not Proof of Love*

Let this sink in:

- You don't need to hold someone tightly to keep them close.

- If they want to leave, your grasp won't stop them.

- If they want to stay, your freedom will invite their trust.

- Control kills connection.

- Real loyalty is not enforced—it's **earned through emotional safety**.

Batman's Code of Devoted Freedom:

1. Love them without gripping.

2. Show up fully, then let them breathe.

3. Don't take space as rejection.

4. Trust that the right ones return, not because they have to—but because they want to.

5. Be the place they *want* to return to—not the cage they feel forced into.

Bonus: Why Freedom Deepens Loyalty

Letting someone breathe doesn't dilute the bond—it *strengthens* it.

Why?

Because when people feel free, they feel safe.

And when they feel safe, they come close.

Willingly. Repeatedly. Joyfully.

Batman doesn't beg for loyalty.

He embodies it.

And that energetic commitment invites others to trust him—even if

they don't always stay close.

Final Reflection

Love is not a leash.

It's not a lock.

It's not a performance you must maintain to be "chosen."

Love—real love—is *quiet consistency.*

It's the kind of loyalty that doesn't panic when someone needs

space.

It's trusting that freedom isn't the end of intimacy—it's the beginning of *authentic connection.*

Batman shows up.

Loyal. Unleashed. Unafraid.

And in doing so, he becomes *the very place others want to return to.*

Reflection Zone

Cat vs. Human Comparison Chart

Situation	Batman's Way	Typical Human Behaviour
Loving someone	Chooses them daily, without pressure	Tries to lock it down or define constantly
Responding to distance	Waits calmly, doesn't panic	Assumes rejection, spirals emotionally
Expressing devotion	Shows up consistently, doesn't cling	Performs loyalty loudly, inconsistently
Navigating freedom in relationships	Trusts, doesn't control	Monitors, questions, gets anxious
Handling insecurity	Holds steady, remains soft	Demands reassurance or withdraws love

Thought Prompts & Journaling Cues

Do I trust love when it's quiet—or do I look for dramatic proof?

Have I ever tried to earn loyalty through control?

What does freedom within connection feel like to me?

Can I stay steady even when I feel unsure—like Batman does?

Am I someone others can feel safe with, even when they need space?

Invitation:

> **<u>Batman Practice:</u>**
>
> Reflect on a relationship where you've felt tempted to grip too tightly.
>
> What would it look like to stay present—but not possessive?
>
> Practice being someone others return to because it feels safe, not because they're afraid to leave.

Chapter 12: You're Still My Favourite Spot

Where Batman Shows Us That Real Love is Chosen—Not Once, But Always

> - *"It's not the drama that keeps me coming back.*
> *It's the calm. It's the you-ness of you.*
> *You're still my favorite spot—even on the quiet days."*
> *— Batman, Emotional Stability in Cat Form*

After all the flirty blinks, the dramatic walkaways, the paw swats

and rooftop serenades, there comes a time in every love story when

the fireworks settle.

And what's left?

A quiet bowl shared in silence.

A spot on the ledge where two tails hang in parallel.

A slow blink, not as a grand gesture, but a gentle "Still here."

Batman knows this stage.

He's lived it a dozen times over with every member of the feline feminine.

And with me.

There are no surprises anymore.

He knows who hisses, who tolerates, who flops dramatically, and who eats first.

And yet—**he still comes back.**

To the same corner. The same bowls. The same rhythms.

Because real love isn't about novelty.

It's about **returning.**

And *choosing* again.

And again.

And again.

The Myth of Forever Sparkles

Humans are obsessed with "keeping the spark alive."

But often, that obsession leads to:

- Manufactured excitement

- Emotional chaos mistaken for passion

- Self-sabotage the moment things feel "too calm"

We panic when the fireworks fade.

We fear the softness.

We confuse *peace* with *boredom*.

But Batman knows—**the spark isn't gone. It's just become warm embers.**

And that? That's where real intimacy lives.

Human Takeaway: ***Love is a Daily Choice, Not a One-Time Declaration***

Romanticized culture teaches us that love is about grand gestures.

The big "I do."

The rom-com kiss in the rain.

The anniversary trip to Bali.

But the truth?

- It's the hand held every morning.

- The text that says "home?"

- The shared silence that feels more comfortable than any words.

- The small, almost invisible act of returning—without fanfare.

Batman returns to his favourite spot **not because he has to—but because he wants to.**

And that's the kind of love that lasts.

Batman's Forever Love Practices:

1. Return, even when nothing's new.

2. Choose presence, even when things are quiet.

3. Notice the familiar, and treat it like magic.

4. Don't chase intensity. Nourish consistency.

5. Let your loyalty be felt—not performed.

Long-Term Love Isn't About Always Feeling "In Love"

It's about:

- Feeling safe

- Feeling seen

- Feeling chosen

- Feeling calm in each other's orbit

Batman doesn't love because it's exciting.

He loves because **it's rooted**.

And rooted love doesn't waver with weather.

It weathers it all.

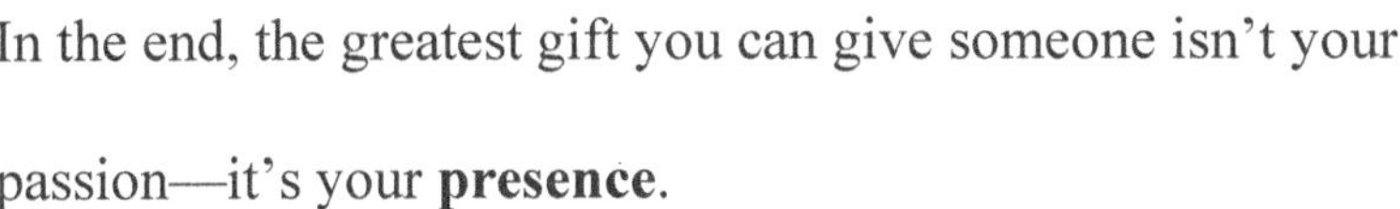

Final Reflection

In the end, the greatest gift you can give someone isn't your passion—it's your **presence**.

It's not being the loudest in the room.

It's being the **one who always comes back to the room**.

Again. And again. And again.

Batman teaches us that true love isn't about chasing new places.

It's about becoming someone's favourite spot.

And staying that way—not because you're perfect.

But because you're consistent.

Still soft. Still near.

Still blinking slowly… even on a Tuesday.

Reflection Zone

Cat vs. Human Comparison Chart

Situation	Batman's Way	Typical Human Behaviour
Long-term love	Returns daily, quietly, with presence	Takes love for granted or seeks novelty
Showing consistency	Same soft blink, same ledge, same time	Inconsistency disguised as spontaneity
Navigating routine	Finds comfort in ritual and rhythm	Complains of boredom, craves drama
Expressing affection over time	Stays near, even when it's not exciting	Withholds love unless there's attention
Choosing love again and again	Doesn't need words—just returns	Needs validation to stay committed

Thought Prompts & Journaling Cues

What does "choosing someone again" look like in my life?

Have I ever mistaken peace for boredom in a relationship?

Where can I bring more consistency into how I love?

Am I offering soft, dependable presence—or expecting grand gestures?

What do I consider my "favourite spots" in love—and do I show up there often enough?

Invitation:

Batman Practice:

Revisit someone—or something—
you love deeply.

Show up today in a small, ordinary
way: a message, a glance, a silent
presence.

Don't perform. Don't declare. Just
return.

And notice how being someone's
favourite spot doesn't take
perfection.

Just consistency, curiosity, and calm.

Chapter 13: Ask Batman – A Feline's Guide to Human Drama

Real Letters. Imaginary People. Too-Real Problems.

-    *"If you have to ask whether it's love or control… it's control."*
— Batman, casually sipping rainwater off a leaf

Dear Batman,

My boyfriend used to slow blink at me all the time when we first

started dating. Now, all he does is scroll through reels with dead eyes. Is the magic gone?

— Heartbroken in Hyderabad

Dear Heartbroken,

Slow blinks are sacred. They're a ritual. If your partner replaced soulful eye contact with zombie-scrolling, the issue isn't the magic—it's the **mindful presence.**

Look him in the eye, blink slowly, and see what happens.

If he blinks back, there's hope.

If he asks if you've got something in your eye, blink twice and walk away like Daisy.

Dear Batman,

Every time I say I need space, my partner takes it personally and sulks. How do I explain that I'm not abandoning him?

— Smothered in Surat

Dear Smothered,

Tell him you're not leaving the room—you're just adjusting the air conditioning.

Space isn't distance. It's oxygen.

And anyone who confuses breathing room

with abandonment needs to sit with

Chairman Mao. She'll teach him boundaries

in under five seconds.

Dear Batman,

He said he needed time to "figure things out." It's been eight months and he still likes my stories but won't reply to my messages. Is this a vibe or a no?

— Confused in Kolkata

Dear Confused,

Girl. That's not a vibe. That's an emotional breadcrumb.

Unfollow. Un-vibe. Reclaim your purring energy.

If he wants to figure things out, he can do it from the spiritual

safety of your blocked list.

Dear Batman,

My partner is loving but also controlling. He decides where we go,

when we meet, even what I post. He says it's because he "loves me too much." Should I be worried?

— Red Flagged in Rajkot

Dear Red,

Love isn't supposed to feel like a leash.

It's supposed to feel like a sun patch on the

floor—you can stretch, roll, and relax in it.

Control disguised as care is still control.

Daisy wouldn't put up with that. Neither should you.

Dear Batman,

I think I'm the problem. I keep chasing people who don't want me

and ignoring those who do. Help me.

— Emotionally Crosswired in Chennai

Dear Crosswired,

Classic tail-chase syndrome. Very human.

Slow down. Sit still. Let affection come to you like sunlight—

don't sprint after shadows.

And remember: The ones who come when you're calm are the ones who'll stay when you're vulnerable.

Chapter 14: The Boyfriend Audit – A Feline-Inspired Checklist

How Batman Would Rate Your Emotional Maturity (and Theirs)

> - *"Before you demand loyalty, check if you're even emotionally pettable."*
> — *Batman, mid-slow blink*

Rate yourself (or your human boyfriend / girlfriend) with a

slow blink or hiss for each statement:

1. I blink slowly instead of sending 17 texts when I feel insecure.

2. I know the difference between giving space and giving the silent treatment.

3. I can handle rejection without becoming a ghost, a jerk, or a guilt-ninja.

4. I don't confuse passion with chaos.

5. I show up consistently—on Mondays *and* on meltdown days.

6. I let people come to me instead of trying to emotionally herd them like cattle.

7. I respond to emotional cues, not just words.

8. I value trust more than territory.

9. I offer affection without an agenda.

10. I know that love means being the safest presence in the room—not the loudest.

Scoring key:

- **8–10 Slow Blinks:** You're basically Batman. Proceed to purr.

- **5–7 Flicking Tail:** You're emotionally aware but still learning the fine art of chill.

- **0–4 Hisses:** You need this book. Read it again. Maybe twice.

HOW TO TRAIN
YOUR HUMAN

Chapter 15: Batman's Love Laws – 10 Unshakable Principles of Conscious Courtship

The Final Word from a Furry Master of Love

- *"My love is silent, steady, and consent-based. Yours should be too."*

— Batman, from the Inner Meowment Temple

Batman's 10 Love Laws

1. **Slow Blink First.** Always offer safety before seeking closeness.

2. **Wait Near the Door—Don't Knock It Down.**

3. **Read the Tail, Not Just the Talk.**

4. **Never Ghost. Just Glide Away Gracefully.**

5. **Space is Sacred. Let Them Miss You.**

6. **Return Without Drama. Stay Without Pressure.**

7. **Purring > Performing.**

8. **Hold Steady, Even When Rejected.**

9. **Love Without Leashing.**

10. **Choose Them Again. And Again.**

    Especially on the boring days.

And there we are—**from whisker to wisdom, from meow to mantra**, Batman has taught us what no dating app, no therapist, and no zodiac meme ever could:

That love is a quiet commitment.

A gentle presence.

A choice made over and over again.

He didn't need words.

He had *paws*.

And presence.

And the kind of patience that turns even the wildest heart into a home.

Epilogue

And Still, He Comes Back

There's something about the way Batman walks.

It's not just the glide, the tail-flick timing, or the silent command of space.

It's the **energy**.

The quiet assurance of someone who doesn't chase, doesn't retreat—just **arrives**.

Over and over again.

No matter how many hisses he's dodged.

No matter how many days he's spent waiting by a closed door.

No matter how often the world has felt distant, chaotic, or unwilling to meet him halfway…

He still comes back.

Not because he's desperate.

Not because he has nowhere else to go.

But because he **chooses** to. Every single day.

And in that choice lies everything we misunderstand about love.

It isn't loud.

It isn't instant.

It doesn't need to be earned or chased or proven through a storm of grand gestures.

Sometimes, love is just a cat who appears outside your door at 6:57 PM—

again.

And again.

And again.

Still soft. Still silent.

Still offering presence, not pressure.

Still choosing you.

You may not have Batman in your life.

But you can **be** Batman.

In how you love. In how you show up. In how you sit beside someone instead of fixing them.

In how you give space. Hold space.

And wait—not with tension, but with trust.

In how you let people roam, knowing that what's true always finds its way back.

Not because you chased it.

But because you became the kind of love worth returning to.

So go ahead.

Slow blink.

Stroll gently.

And become someone's favourite spot—

not by being perfect…

…but by always coming back with kindness in your heart and grace in your paws.

With purrs, presence, and all my love,

Rashmie

And her furry relationship guru,

Batman

Bonus: Outtakes & Bloopers from the Casanova Chronicles

Because Even the Best Boyfriend Gets Slapped Sometimes

> - *"No cats were emotionally harmed during the making of this book.*
> *Slightly humiliated? Yes. But mostly fed."*
> — *Rashmie, Head of Treat Distribution*

Scene: Batman attempts a rooftop serenade.

He strikes a pose.

He slow-blinks at Daisy.

He meows, once—softly.

She responds by *knocking over the water bowl and flouncing off like a furry soap opera villain.*

Batman stares at the spilled water.

Takes one sip.

Carries on.

Scene: Chairman Mao gives Batman a rare nuzzle.

He leans in.

She headbutts him.

For a full 1.5 seconds, it's tender.

Then she bites his ear and struts away like she's just dropped a mic.

He blinks once. Resets his jaw. Does not press charges.

Scene: Maple eats from Batman's bowl.

He watches. Tail still.

She finishes, walks away.

He walks up to the empty bowl, sniffs it…

…then walks away like a disappointed Michelin inspector.

Scene: Batman tries to jump onto a ledge mid-slow blink.

Misses.

Lands in flower pot.

Looks directly at me like, *"You saw nothing."*

Scene: Rashmie tries to pet Batman before he's ready.

Batman: "Nice try, human."

Walks off dramatically.

Returns 10 minutes later. Rubs against my ankle.

Accepts affection *only* when he initiates it. Diva level: 10/10.

Mini-Batman Dictionary (Because Yes, He Has Moods)

- **The Glare & Blink Combo** – Used when someone takes his spot. Translates to: "Excuse me. I had *reservations*."

- **The Turn-Around-Sit-Facing-Away Pose** – Often directed at Maple. Means: "I acknowledge your existence but will not validate your behaviour."

- **Tail-Twitching While Eating** – Indicates mild irritation but unwillingness to stop dinner.

- **Sudden Lick-Then-Leave** – Emotional confusion or secret affection. Unconfirmed.

Deleted Chapter Titles That Didn't Make the Cut (But Kinda Slap):

- *"The Paw-sitive Power of Selective Attention"*

- *"Love, But Make It Aloof"*

- *"How to Stay Present When Everyone Else is Chasing Tail"*

- *"Hissed But Not Broken: A Feline's Guide to Rejection Recovery"*

- *"Dating Apps? I Have Terracotta Ledges."*

And with that, our Cat Casanova exits stage left.

Not with a meow. Not with drama.

But with a slow blink and a slightly judgmental tail flick.

Fade to purr.

Paw-sibly not the end. He will return after dinner.